INDIAN STYLE POSTCARDS

Suzanne Slesin □ Stafford Cliff □ David Brittain

Chronicle Books • San Francisco

Copyright © 1990 by Suzanne Slesin
and Stafford Cliff. All rights reserved.
No part of this book may be reproduced in any form without written
permission from the publisher.

Printed in Japan

Design: Julie Noyes
Editorial: Karen Kligerman

A note to the correspondent: These
slightly oversized postcards require
the same postage as a first-class letter.

ISBN: 0-87701-772-7

Distributed in Canada by Raincoast
Books, 112 East Third Avenue,
Vancouver, B.C. V5T 1C8

10 9 8 7 6 5 4 3 2 1

Chronicle Books
275 Fifth Street
San Francisco, California 94103

INTRODUCTION

India is a country with a population of 800 million, thousands of gods, hundreds of castes, and myriad languages. It is, therefore, somewhat problematic to attempt to define a single Indian style. Rather, it would be wiser to speak in terms of the piety and spirituality that seem to unify the people of this vast and contradictory landscape.

A fantastic world of demons and ghosts, gods and heroes, reaches into the mundane lives of most Indians. Amidst the teeming street scenes with their profusion of hawkers, beggars, merchants, worshippers, and holy men resides an intricate sense of ceremony. There is a sacredness attached to everything—from a simple bathing ritual to the observance of mystical rites.

While Indian spirituality acts as a unifying force, Indian architecture reflects a variety of eclectic traditions. Churches in the south bear the imprint of Spain and Portugal; forts and ramparts of Rajasthan have drawn from the magnificence of ancient Persia; and the huge overhanging roofs and open spaces of a maharaja's teak palace reflect the influence of Chinese tradition.

Some contemporary homes have incorporated western furniture and knickknacks. These American and European touches combined with exotic eastern influences such as brilliant colors and exuberant patterns can sometimes lend a playful confusion to interiors that strive to be modern. But the hand of progress and urbanization cannot suppress the ubiquitous reminders of India's pure and sacred past, most faithfully embodied in the people themselves.

Lofty pine trees and an English-style flower-bordered walkway frame a small bungalow in Simla.

From *Indian Style Postcards,* copyright © 1990 by Suzanne Slesin and Stafford Cliff. Photographs by David Brittain. Published by Chronicle Books.

At a farmhouse near Bissau, the two palm impressions
beside the entrance indicate the births of two sons.

From *Indian Style Postcards,* copyright © 1990 by Suzanne
Slesin and Stafford Cliff. Photographs by David Brittain.
Published by Chronicle Books.

Women and girls from a village in Gujarat use their heads to carry vessels of water, which they fetch at sunset from a nearby well.

From *Indian Style Postcards,* copyright © 1990 by Suzanne Slesin and Stafford Cliff. Photographs by David Brittain. Published by Chronicle Books.

The double niche in a kitchen in Jaisalmer includes a tiny window, a small brazier for cooking, and a sparkling collection of brass double-boilers.

From *Indian Style Postcards,* copyright © 1990 by Suzanne Slesin and Stafford Cliff. Photographs by David Brittain. Published by Chronicle Books.

In the village of Hodka, the door to every house is different. This wooden door is decorated with metal cross braces and studs.

From *Indian Style Postcards,* copyright © 1990 by Suzanne Slesin and Stafford Cliff. Photographs by David Brittain. Published by Chronicle Books.

The monastery at Lamayuru in the Himalayas is ringed with fields of barley.

From *Indian Style Postcards,* copyright © 1990 by Suzanne Slesin and Stafford Cliff. Photographs by David Brittain. Published by Chronicle Books.

Chettinad House, a Beaux-Arts palace outside Madras, has a panoramic view of the Ayadar River.

From *Indian Style Postcards,* copyright © 1990 by Suzanne Slesin and Stafford Cliff. Photographs by David Brittain. Published by Chronicle Books.

Bungas, or round huts, have for centuries been a popular form for houses in the Kutch area of the Thar Desert because their round shape exposes less surface to the elements.

From *Indian Style Postcards,* copyright © 1990 by Suzanne Slesin and Stafford Cliff. Photographs by David Brittain. Published by Chronicle Books.

A flower vendor sails with his wares out on Dal Lake in Kashmir.

From *Indian Style Postcards,* copyright © 1990 by Suzanne Slesin and Stafford Cliff. Photographs by David Brittain. Published by Chronicle Books.

This door and facade display the flat, stylized, and geometric designs often found in the desert towns of Baramsar and Roopsi.

From *Indian Style Postcards,* copyright © 1990 by Suzanne Slesin and Stafford Cliff. Photographs by David Brittain. Published by Chronicle Books.

In India, the elephant has always been venerated as a sacred animal and a symbol of royalty. Carvings of elephants appear on capitals, ornamental brackets, and keystones.

From *Indian Style Postcards,* copyright © 1990 by Suzanne Slesin and Stafford Cliff. Photographs by David Brittain. Published by Chronicle Books.

Throughout India, the unrestrained use of color is a pervasive theme in the exterior decoration of houses, as in this bright coral building with aqua doors and shutters.

From *Indian Style Postcards,* copyright © 1990 by Suzanne Slesin and Stafford Cliff. Photographs by David Brittain. Published by Chronicle Books.

Distinctive white freehand designs on ocher-colored walls are traditional decorations in the small desert villages on the Pakistan border.

From *Indian Style Postcards,* copyright © 1990 by Suzanne Slesin and Stafford Cliff. Photographs by David Brittain. Published by Chronicle Books.

The immense palace of Umaid Bhawan outside Jodhpur synthesizes Art Deco with the romantic style of old India.

From *Indian Style Postcards,* copyright © 1990 by Suzanne Slesin and Stafford Cliff. Photographs by David Brittain. Published by Chronicle Books.

A bathroom in a nineteenth-century palace outside Jodhpur has been redesigned to look as if it were part of an ancient grotto.

From *Indian Style Postcards,* copyright © 1990 by Suzanne Slesin and Stafford Cliff. Photographs by David Brittain. Published by Chronicle Books.

In an apartment near New Delhi, a Chinese painting on glass of a Peshwa dignitary hangs above three polychrome figurines of soldiers.

From *Indian Style Postcards*, copyright © 1990 by Suzanne Slesin and Stafford Cliff. Photographs by David Brittain. Published by Chronicle Books.

In Churu, Rajasthan, painted scenes from the lives of Ganesha and Krishna top the colored glass fanlights of an apartment building.

From *Indian Style Postcards,* copyright © 1990 by Suzanne Slesin and Stafford Cliff. Photographs by David Brittain. Published by Chronicle Books.

The mud walls of a farmhouse near Bissau are renewed each year at festival times. The pottery jars are for carrying and storing water.

From *Indian Style Postcards,* copyright © 1990 by Suzanne Slesin and Stafford Cliff. Photographs by David Brittain. Published by Chronicle Books.

The natural colors of materials such as terra-cotta tile and red Indian sandstone are juxtaposed with vibrant paints in a variety of inventive designs for building facades.

From *Indian Style Postcards,* copyright © 1990 by Suzanne Slesin and Stafford Cliff. Photographs by David Brittain. Published by Chronicle Books.

A grain truck, waiting to be loaded at Cochin, displays the brilliantly colored hand-painted decorations typical of the state of Kerala.

From *Indian Style Postcards,* copyright © 1990 by Suzanne Slesin and Stafford Cliff. Photographs by David Brittain. Published by Chronicle Books.

Stairs lead to a landing with an unusual Chinese-Chippendale railing in a house in Cochin.

From *Indian Style Postcards,* copyright © 1990 by Suzanne Slesin and Stafford Cliff. Photographs by David Brittain. Published by Chronicle Books.

The antique brass-studded doors contrast with the appliquéd window shades of a house on the outskirts of New Delhi.

From *Indian Style Postcards*, copyright © 1990 by Suzanne Slesin and Stafford Cliff. Photographs by David Brittain. Published by Chronicle Books.